THE
FLYING GEESE QUILT

Other books by the authors
The Lone Star Quilt Handbook
Trip Around The World Quilts
The Boston Commons Quilt

Front cover: *Flying Geese* wall quilt by Blanche Young.
Back cover: (upper left) Wall quilt by Blanche Young.
(upper right) Miniature quilt by Jeannette Cole,
"Blanche" doll by Marie White and Carolyn Reese.
(lower left and right) *Flying Geese* quilt by Jewel
Patterson.

THE
FLYING GEESE QUILT

Blanche Young & Helen Young

Acknowledgements

Our heartfelt thanks to the many friends that helped make this book possible; to Kaye Rheingans for her technical advice; and to Jane Haxton, Sheila Anderson, Sherry Schneider, Pat Gilbert, Doris Crutchfield, and Debbie Gordon for contributing parts of their homes and so much more to the photography sessions.

Our gratitude to those that sent their Flying Geese quilts "flying" to us: Jewel Patterson of Houston, Texas; Richard and Janet Allen of Alfred, Maine; Laverne Mathews of Orange, Texas; Mary Lu Stark of Albuquerque, New Mexico; and Diana Leone of Santa Clara, California.

A special thanks to Mike Schneider for providing us with the only real goose among a flock of fabric ones.

The help and support from our family is greatly appreciated.

Photographs by Tom Rizzo and Jeff Frank,
   Color Image Systems, Riverside, California
Diagrams and illustrations by Helen Young

Published by C&T Publishing
P.O. Box 1456
Lafayette, CA 94549

ISBN: 0-914881-13-2

Contents

Introduction

The Quilts

Introduction

The *Flying Geese* quilt is a traditional favorite among quilters. The easily recognized design is known by different names; *Wild Goose Chase, Wild Geese Flying, Geese in Flight* among them. The reason for the name is apparent; how logical for an early quilt-maker to use the simple triangle to represent the shape of geese against the sky.

We have noticed a renewed interest in the *Flying Geese* quilt. Everywhere we've traveled, we have seen outstanding new quilts that have the flavor of the old traditional *Flying Geese* quilts. We don't know whether the recent resurgence of this quilt pattern is due to the current availability of striped fabrics, or simply because quilters are rising to the challenge of combining the many fabrics that give these quilts their character.

We have applied some of the same concepts and methods that we presented in *The Lone Star Quilt Handbook* and *Trip Around The World Quilts*. The major difference is that in the *Flying Geese* quilt the triangles still must be sewn individually. Even so, our idea of a multiple template can be applied successfully. We have researched each step of the quilts construction and give suggestions and options for each. Our approach is not that different, but we do offer some timesaving techniques.

We do list suggested yardage amounts for each quilt but have also included a Yardage Chart. The quilt-maker can then design a masterpiece quilt with an unlimited number of fabrics.

We have included complete instructions for the *Flying Geese* quilt in all sizes, from a miniature quilt to a king size one. The directions for the variation of *Wild Goose Chase* are also included.

So gather together a flock of fabrics, in a gaggle of colors, and enjoy making your *Flying Geese* quilt!

Supplies

Markers These can be anything that will mark on fabric and will not run or bleed. Regular pencils, colored pencils, dressmakers chalk pencils and felt tip markers are some of the things we use. Always test markers by writing on a scrap of fabric and wetting it.

Ruler Use a 6 inch or 12 inch ruler and a yardstick or tape measure.

Scissors Several layers of fabric will be cut together, so a very good, sharp pair of scissors is a necessity. Use paper scissors to cut the template.

Pins Extra long, glass headed pins work the best.

Thread Use cotton covered polyester or polyester thread in a color that blends with most of the fabrics. A medium shade of gray or tan is a good choice.

Spray Starch Spray starch all fabrics while pressing for better results during marking, cutting and sewing.

Needles Use quilting needles (betweens) in sizes 8, 9, 10 or 12. Baste with sharps or milliners' needles.

Batting Purchase batting either in packages (sold by the quilt size) or by the yard.

Frames/Hoops Many different styles of hoops and frames are available. If a hoop is used, the quilt must first be basted together.

Sewing Machine This technique is developed for machine piecing.

Fabrics & Design

Fabrics

The *Flying Geese* quilt offers an opportunity to the quilter to mix prints and colors as never before! Big prints, little prints, bright and dark, they can all be combined with wonderful results in a *Flying Geese* quilt. Whether you are selecting all new fabrics at the local quilt shop or using some of your own collection, here are some hints and ideas about fabrics to consider.

Use broadcloth weight, woven all cotton or cotton/polyester fabrics. Avoid loosely woven, flimsy fabrics and any that fray easily. Look for an interesting assortment of prints. Anything can go in these quilts; dots, stripes, paisleys, and all sizes of florals.

Exactly how many different fabrics to use is entirely up to you. Virginia Nicholson's quilt (Plate 3) has 15 combinations, or 30 fabrics, while Janet Allen has used over 300 fabrics in her quilt (Plate 2).

The more fabrics you use, the less you will need of each. Those pieces that are too small for anything else can finally be put to good use. The quilt on the cover, made from scraps, has 12 combinations, or only 24 fabrics, yet the assortment of prints gives the appearance of many more.

Don't feel that only a full scrapbag will give these quilts charm. The quilts in Plate 4 and on the back cover (lower left) were made with all new fabrics yet they have an antique look to them.

The proportions of light and dark fabrics will determine the overall effect of the quilt. The soft effect of Verna Brightwell's quilt in Plate 10 is achieved with light and medium shades and a light stripe. The dramatic effect of the quilt in Plate 16 is caused by mixing dark and medium fabrics against a very dark stripe.

Although the colors in the stripe usually dictate the color scheme of the quilt, you can control the proportion of each color. Jewel Patterson's quilt on the back cover (lower left) has a majority of rust fabrics; the light and dark greens complement. Mary Lu Stark chose mostly blue prints to form the background for both the dark red and the dark blue fabrics in her quilt in Plate 4. Although several aqua fabrics are seen in the quilt in Plate 1, the overall look is that of a brown and rust quilt.

Mixing prints

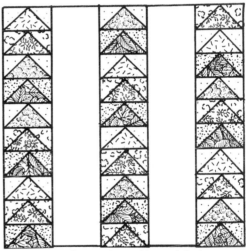

Light and medium fabrics

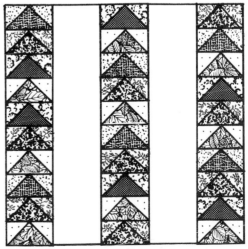

Medium and dark fabrics

When a large number of fabrics are used in a quilt, the amount of each fabric is so small that it is possible to use an outrageous color and have it just add an accent instead of spoiling the color scheme. Sometimes that improbable color is just the right highlight. The pink in the quilt on the cover and the gold that Pamela Toomey used in her wall quilt in Plate 9 are exactly the touch of color needed.

Preshrink all the fabrics and then press, using spray starch.

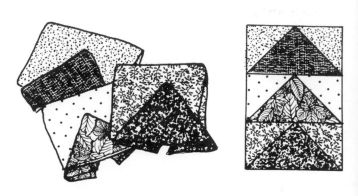

Grouping the fabrics into sets

Design

After the fabrics are chosen, they should be grouped into sets or combinations. One will be the large triangle, and the other will form the background. Loosely fold the fabrics into a triangle and place it against the other to get a better sense of which should be the background. We usually use the darker or brighter of any two fabrics for the "goose" triangle and use the lighter one for the background triangles. The strong graphic appeal of the *Flying Geese* quilt is formed by the large triangle so we try to emphasize it.

Another way to emphasize the large triangles is to use the same background fabric throughout. The quilts on the back cover (lower left) and in Plate 17 use a variety of fabrics for the "geese" and only one for all the background triangles.

We try to have some triangles contrast sharply and have others blend into their backgrounds. To decide which effect you prefer, study the difference between the quilts. Notice the high contrast in the quilts in Plates 2 and 4, and the mix of high contrast and low contrast in the quilts in Plates 1 and 9. Group your fabrics according to the effect you want to achieve.

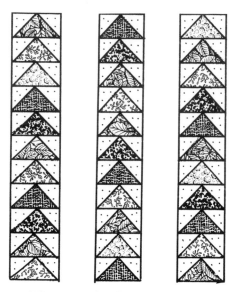

The same background fabric

Different background fabrics

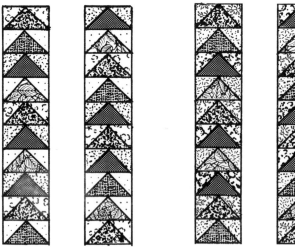

Contrasting the fabrics   *Blending the fabrics*

Cutting both large and background triangles from the same fabric makes it hard to arrange the rows. Even using the same color for some of both can cause problems. If they are next to each other they will form a chevron.

Almost all of the quilts in the color section have random arrangements. There is no precise order in which to place the sewn triangles. Instead, they are joined after being casually arranged into rows. This is what gives these quilts their scrapbag, antique look.

As a variation, the fabrics can be arranged in a certain order, and then repeated in sequence. The quilts in Plates 3 and 5 have planned arrangements of fabrics.

The *Christmas Geese* quilt in Plate 5 also shows another possible variation; the colors of the rows alternate. The color of the rows can also change, as done in *Shadows* (Plate 15).

Another design variation is to change the direction of the flight of the geese. In the antique quilt top in Plate 6, the rows alternate directions. In the *Confused Goose* in Plate 17, the directions of the triangles change within each row.

Stripes

Quilters are enjoying the wealth of repeat strips currently available. No longer are fabric manufacturers thinking only of the home seamstress, they are answering directly to the quiltmaker. Instead of printing only narrow stripes meant for articles of clothing, they are printing wide, ornate border stripes made just for quilts.

Although most stripes will be symmetrical, asymmetrical stripes can also be used. Turn half of the stripes the other direction to make a symmetrical quilt.

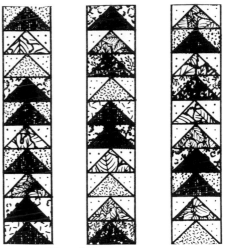

Random arrangement

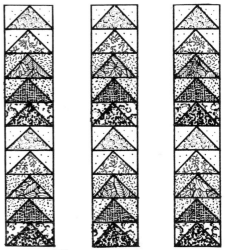

Planned arrangement

Symmetrical stripe

Asymmetrical stripe

Any width of stripe can be used. If a stripe is very narrow, use more than one repeat. We originally felt that the stripe should not be wider than the rows, but we have since realized that many of the antique *Flying Geese* quilts did have wider stripes. The fabric used in the antique top in Plate 6 is wider than the triangles. The width of the stripe will affect the width of the finished quilt. The *Christmas Geese* wall quilt in Plate 5 has almost the same number of the same size of triangles as the wall quilt on the back cover, yet the wider stripe creates an almost square quilt. To keep the quilt a certain size, rows of triangles can be added or eliminated to compensate for narrow or wide stripes.

Many of the striped fabrics now available are printed with three or four different stripe designs across the width. More than one stripe can be used in the *Flying Geese* quilt. Alternate two different stripes, or use a different stripe to border the outer edges as in the quilts in Plates 3 and 4. Laverne, Linda and Betty Mathews have incorporated several different stripes into their delightful *Climbing Flowers Strippy Quilt* in Plate 7.

Something to consider when choosing a stripe is the effect of contrast. We have found when the colors of the stripe blend into the triangles, or if the edge of the stripe is not well-defined, that the "geese won't fly." That is, the triangles will not stand out from the stripe. Using a dark, well-defined stripe will emphasize the triangles as in the wall quilt in Plate 9. You may prefer having equal emphasis on both triangles and stripes. If so, feel free to use more ornate stripes as in the quilts in Plates 5 and 8.

Do not cut out the stripes until the rows are completed. The rows can be placed on the striped fabric to "try on" different stripes. You may find that a different stripe looks better than your original choice.

Many antique *Flying Geese* quilts used a printed fabric instead of stripes. Our antique top on Plate 6 shows this. Janet Allen also used a print in her quilt in Plate 2, since an antique quilt was her inspiration.

You may want to rearrange the design of certain stripes to make them more effective. A stripe that lacks a defined edge can have a narrow stripe sewn to it. Stripes can also be made by sewing narrow stripes to a printed fabric.

Stripes blending into the rows

Well-defined stripes emphasizing the rows

Equal emphasis on stripe and row

Creating a stripe

12

Sewing Techniques

Although the sewing machine makes it possible to piece a quilt in a fraction of the time needed for hand piecing, it also creates problems that would not be encountered in hand sewing. When beginning a line of stitching, small pieces or sharp points tend to catch in the feed mechanism of the sewing machine. It is also difficult to maintain a consistent seam allowance at the end of each seam since as the piece tapers into a point, there is not enough fabric on one side to be fed through evenly. These problems can be solved by eliminating the points of the triangles' seam allowances. This will make them easier to sew and there will be no trimming later.

Even though the triangles are individually sewn, we chose to apply our multiple template concept to the *Flying Geese* quilt. This will eliminate the errors and distortion that can be caused by tracing and moving one template over and over again. The multiple template will mark a row of triangles with a minimum of moving and distortion. Cut out the templates on the outer lines, removing the notches.

Arrange the fabrics into sets, or combinations. Separate the fabrics for the large triangles from the background fabrics. Layer them in corresponding order. If the fabrics are layered in order, they will not have to be rearranged before sewing.

The fabrics should be layered in groups of 5 or 6 fabrics. Because some of the cutting is on the bias, we don't try to cut any more than that at a time. Always try to have a light colored fabric or one with a simple print as the top layer. It will be easier to see the marks. Any scraps or odd shaped pieces can be placed between the full pieces for cutting.

Square the fabric by drawing a line perpendicular to the selvage. Use an L-square ruler or anything with a true right angle. Place the template against this line and ½ inch away from the selvage.

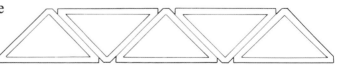

Multiple templates

Marking

Mark the edges of the template and in the notches. Trace the template, end to end, across the width of the fabric. Turn the template to match the previously marked triangles. Use a common line when marking the next row. After the outer edges of the template are traced, use a ruler and draw lines connecting the notches. These will also be cutting lines.

In the instructions for each quilt, we refer to the number of rows to cut of each fabric. Tracing the template twice across the fabric equals one row, as shown. Putting two sided tape, or a loop of regular tape, on the back of the template will hold it in place while tracing around it.

The width of fabric will produce more large triangles than background triangles. Instead of listing separate fabric requirements for each of the two sizes of triangles, we have based the yardage amounts on the number of units (one large triangle with two background triangles) that the widths of the fabrics will yield. This will allow you to purchase the fabrics and later decide which ones will be used for the large or the background triangles.

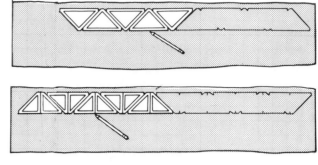

Marking the fabrics

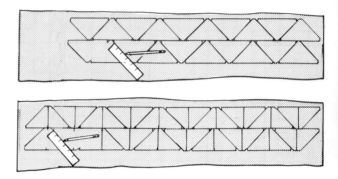

Connecting the notches

Pinning

Pin in the center of each triangle before cutting. The pins in the background triangles can be used as grain line guides. Pin on the lengthwise grain with the point of the pin towards the point of the triangle. The head of the pin will be towards the right angle. After the triangles are cut apart, they are stacked with the pins pointing the same direction. This will keep the grain lines consistent. It is too easy to turn a triangle a quarter turn and have the grain line going crosswise. This would be noticeable with a stripe or a one-way print. The finished rows will also handle better if the edges are on the lengthwise grain.

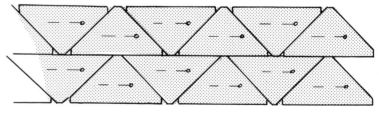

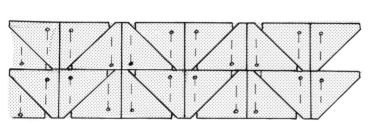

Pinning the background triangles

Cutting

Cut the rows apart, keeping the scissors straight. Cut the triangles apart on the diagonal lines. Trim off the tips or notches.

Turn the background triangles so the pins all point the same directions. Keep the groups separate by placing them in a shallow box or a small plastic bag. After all the work of deciding which background went with which fabric, you don't want them to get mixed up now!

Remove the pins as you sew, making sure the fabrics stay in order.

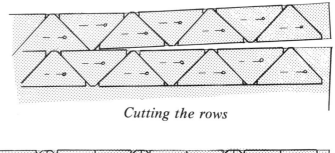

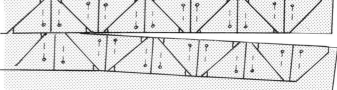

Cutting the rows

The instructions for each quilt include the number of rows to mark and the amount of fabric to purchase if only one background fabric is used. Fold the fabric in fourths to enable you to cut more than one layer at a time.

The yardage amounts in the instructions for each quilt allow for extra units. There may be some fabric combinations that are not effective, or perhaps there may be a color that needs to be only an accent. Having extra units of each combination will allow you to use less of some and more of other combinations. Also, if any mistakes are made in the sewing, those units can simply be discarded.

Cutting the diagonal lines

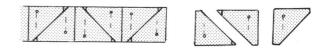

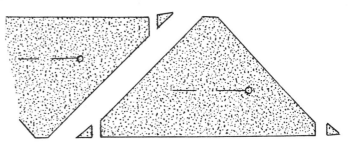

Trimming the points

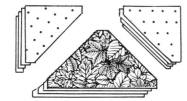

Stacking the triangles right side up

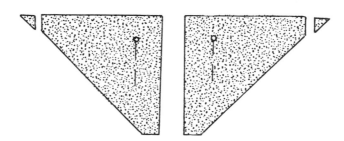

Sewing

Always sew with a consistent ¼ inch seam allowance, using 12 to 15 stitches per inch. There is no need for backstitching at this stage since the seams do not pull apart easily, being on the diagonal. We are offering three different methods for joining the triangles.

Place the pinned stacks to the right hand side of the sewing machine where they will not be disrupted. Place them right sides up as shown on the previous page. We prefer to sew one stack at a time, removing the pins from each stack as we sew.

Method 1—Both background triangles are sewn to the large triangle in one continuous line of stitching. Place a background triangle on the large triangle, matching the edges and sew from edge to edge. Lift up the needle and presser foot and pull the piece away from the presser foot slightly. Open, then place the other background triangle in position and continue sewing. Each piece is handled only once.

Sew the next set the same way without clipping the threads between. There will be a chain of completed units.

Method 2—This method also uses chain piecing. All the left-hand background pieces are sewn to the large triangles. They are clipped apart, then the right-hand background triangles are added. This is the most time efficient method.

Method 3—This method is to be used with the most stubborn of sewing machines. If your machine insists on catching the tips of the triangles and pulling them down through the hole in the throat plate, the only thing to do is begin sewing at a larger edge. Place the right-hand background piece on the large triangle and sew from the top to the bottom. These can be chain pieced. After they are clipped apart, they must be turned over, with the other background piece on the bottom, to again sew from the top to the bottom of the large triangle.

When using either Method 1 or 2, the units should be clipped apart in order. This will make it easier when adding the second background triangles.

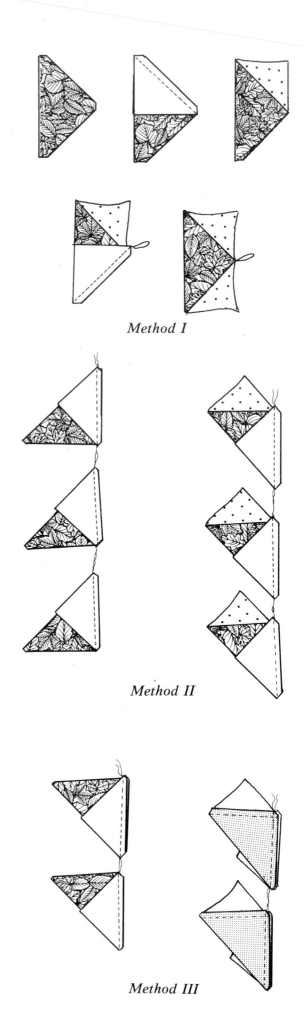

Method I

Method II

Method III

1 *Flying Geese* quilt (92″ × 100″) by Blanche Young. This is a random arrangement of over 40 fabrics.

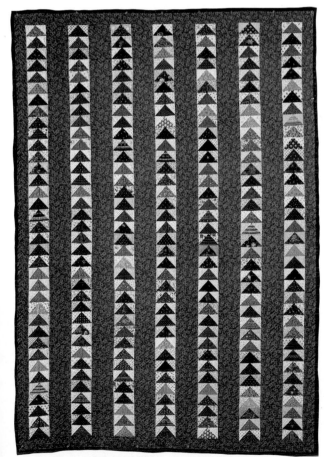

2 *A Goose Flying* (64″ × 94″) by Janet Allen. This quilt contains over 300 fabrics. It was made as a gift for her husband, Richard Allen.

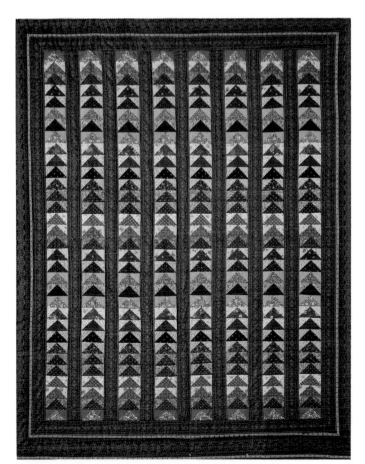

3 *Flying Geese* quilt (89″ × 97″) by Virginia Nicholson. Fifteen fabrics are repeated in sequence.

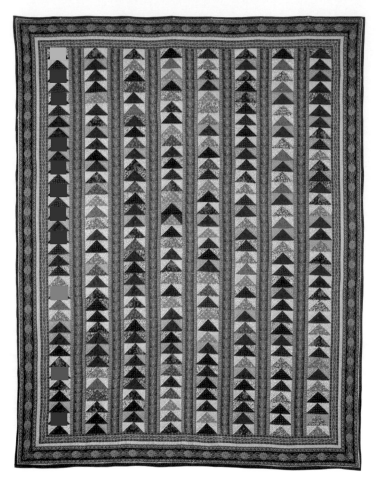

5 *Christmas Geese* (35″ × 32″) by Helen Young. Six green and six red fabrics are repeated in sequence.

4 *Flying Geese* quilt (76″ × 100″) by Maggie Bynum. Fabrics were selected by quilt owner Mary Lu Stark.

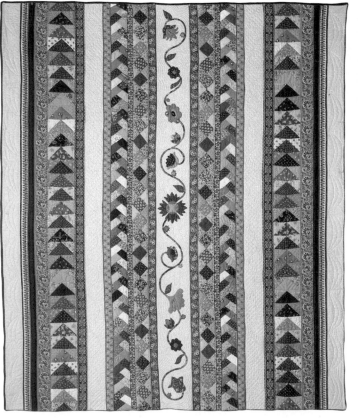

6 Antique quilt tops owned by Lynette Bingham and Blanche Young.

7 *Climbing Flowers Strippy Quilt* (72″ × 88″) by Laverne Mathews, Linda Mathews, and Betty Mathews. Quilted by Celia Ardoin. Owned by Wanda Morris. An original design with Flying Geese as an accent.

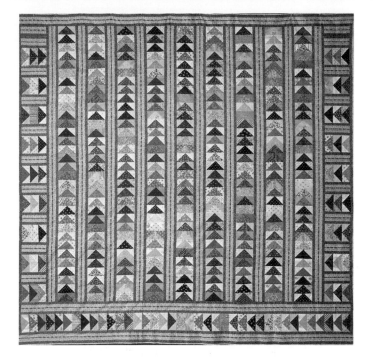

8 *Baby Flying Geese* (36″ × 44″) by Helen Young. Miniature quilt (15″ × 18″) by Jeannette Cole.

10 (upper right) *Flying Geese* quilt (99″ × 91″) by Verna Brightwell.

11 (center right) *Wild Goose Chase* wall quilt (30″ × 16″) by Mary Andra Holmes.

12 (lower right) Antique *Wild Goose Chase* quilt owned by Helen Young.

9 *Flying Geese* wall quilt (30″ × 30″) by Pamela Toomey.

14 *Goin' South* (36″ × 24″) by Helen Young. Rust triangles represent geese migrating south for the winter.

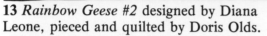

13 *Rainbow Geese #2* designed by Diana Leone, pieced and quilted by Doris Olds.

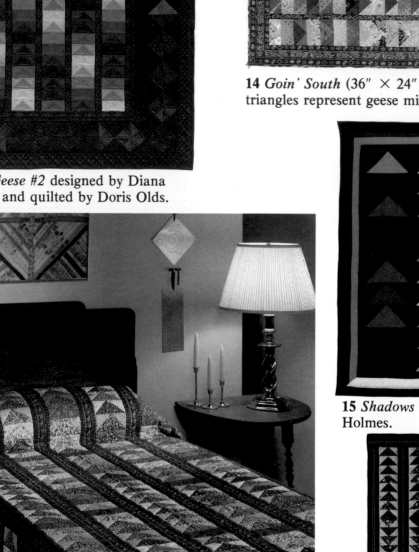

15 *Shadows* (18″ × 18″) by Mary Andra Holmes.

16 (above) *Flying Geese* quilt (72″ × 96″) by Blanche Young.

17 (right) *Confused Goose* quilt (46″ × 82″) by Blanche Young.

Pressing

There are also some different options to consider when pressing. The seams can face the large triangles, or the background, or be pressed open.

Pressing the seams towards the large triangle will help it stand out from the background. The seams will also be towards the darker fabric, so the seam allowances will not show through. If you intend to outline the large triangle with quilting, it will be better to have them this way.

Pressing the seams towards the background will make it easier to sew the rows together. The joining seams will cross the two previous seams exactly.

Pressing the seams open is not customary in patchwork. We find it works well with the tiniest of pieces, such as the $1'' \times 2''$ triangles used in the miniature quilt.

If the triangles are sewn with Method 1, finger press the seam in the right direction before adding the second background piece.

With Methods 2 and 3, press after clipping apart the triangles after the first seam. Either press with an iron, or finger press. Sometimes running a fingernail along the seam is all that is needed.

Forming the Rows

If the quilt has a planned arrangement, the units can be simply sewn together in order. Most *Flying Geese* quilts have random arrangements. It is important to have the lights and darks evenly distributed and to avoid concentrations of one color in an area. We try not to have the same fabric next to each other (across the stripe) but it always manages to happen!

One way to arrange the units is to form each row using some of each fabric. If each row has 20 triangle units, and there are 10 different sets of fabrics, there would be 2 of each fabric in each row. The second row would be arranged next to the first. Each row would be arranged next to the previous ones. It would be possible to rearrange the fabrics one row at a time.

The rows can also be arranged one fabric at a time. Distribute all of one fabric before placing the next. This allows you to place the stronger colors first, and then fill in with the others.

With the bed size quilts, the only surface large enough to accommodate all the units is usually the bed itself.

After all the triangle units are arranged into rows, stack each row, starting from the bottom.

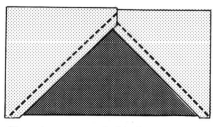

Pressing toward the large triangle

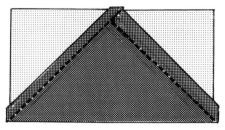

Pressing toward the background

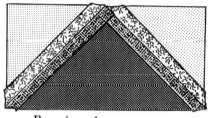

Pressing the seams open

Arranging by row

Stacking the rows

Sew with a consistent ¼ inch seam allowance. If the seams were pressed towards the background, the stitching will cross the seams where they intersect. If the seams were pressed away from the background, use a pin to mark the tip of the large triangle. Do not sew too deeply and sew over the tip of the triangle.

Join the units, starting at the top. The rows can be sewn one at a time or by chain piecing.

To chain piece, place the stacked rows in order from left to right. Sew the first and second triangle units of each row. Do not clip the threads, but continue adding the third unit of each row. It is easier to keep a consistent seam allowance when continuing the sewing like this.

After the rows are completed, the seams should be pressed up so the point of the triangle will lie flat.

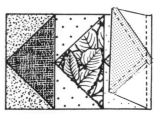

Sewing into rows

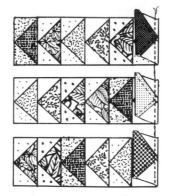

Chain piecing the rows

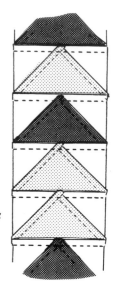

Pressing the rows

Joining the Rows

After pressing, measure or place the rows on top of one another to determine if they are the same length. Even with the most careful attention to marking, cutting and sewing, these rows can be slightly different lengths. Find the average length and cut the stripes that size. The longer rows will be eased in and any shorter ones can be pulled slightly to fit. Never sew the stripe to fit the row; make the row fit the stripe. Cut each stripe at the same part of its design. Allow ¼ inch seam allowances on the sides and ends.

Begin from the left-hand side of the quilt, sewing with the row on the bottom and the stripe on top. This makes it possible to follow the edge of the stripe when sewing. Don't let the underneath seams flip back as they are sewn over.

Pin the next row to the stripe, matching the triangles to the previous row. Although some creeping is inevitable, the triangles should be in a line horizontally across the quilt. In order to follow the stripe, turn the piece over to sew.

Continue to join the rows to the stripes, always sewing with the stripe on top. If the stripe has a one-way design, make sure it follows the same direction.

Press the seams toward the stripes.

Sewing the stripe to the row

Sewing the next rows

Finishing the Quilts

Borders

We prefer finishing the quilt by edging the entire quilt with the same stripe used between the rows. A simple way to enlarge the quilt is to add additional stripes or printed borders.

Mitered borders should be the size of the quilt plus twice the width of the borders. Add ½ inch for seams. Always measure across the center of the quilt, not the outside edges. Stripes with one-way designs can be cut and pieced in the center so the corners will be identical.

Sew the outside borders to the quilt, starting and stopping ¼ inch away from the corners of the quilt. Fold back and crease the border. Sew from the outside corner in towards the quilt. Or instead of machine stitching, simply sew by hand from the front using a blind stitch. It is easier to match the design of the stripe this way.

The quilts in Plates 10 and 16 show a variation to the usual arrangement of rows. The rows were turned on the sides and bottom to exactly follow the shape of the bed. Effects like this can be planned on paper or the rows can be arranged on the bed itself.

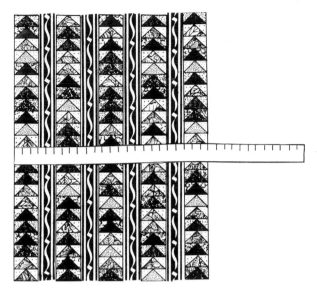

Measuring for outer borders

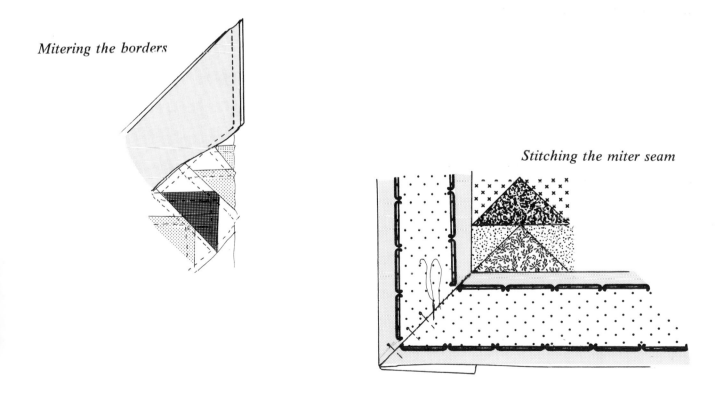

Mitering the borders

Stitching the miter seam

Basting the Quilt

Seam the backing pieces together with ¾ inch seams. Press the seams open after trimming off the selvages. Cut the backing and batting about two inches larger than the quilt top on all sides. Batting should always be removed from the package a day before it is used in order for the folds to relax.

Mark the center of each edge on the quilt top, backing and batting. This will help keep the layers aligned during the basting and quilting.

The quilt should be basted before quilting on a hoop. Spread the backing on a large table. Some of the quilt will drape over the sides. Carefully spread the batting on top. Place the quilt on top, matching the centers of all the edges. Smooth out any fullness.

Baste through the center of both the stripes and the rows. Add horizontal rows every 6 to 8 inches. Use a long, fine needle and quilting thread. Using quilting thread will allow you to use longer pieces of thread with a minimum of tangling.

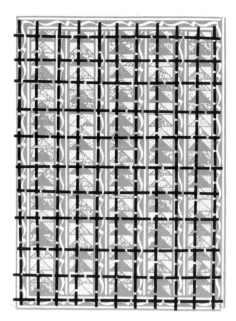

Basting the quilt

Quilting the Quilt

The quilt can be quilted one of several different ways. The most traditional is to quilt ¼ inch from the seams. The triangles can also be simply outlined by quilting around the large triangles. We have found that antique *Flying Geese* quilts often have a line of quilting through the center of the triangles. The antique *Wild Goose Chase* in Plate 12 is quilted this way.

A line of quilting along the stripe will help define it. Quilt the stripes in straight lines or follow the design of the print.

Thread the needle with a single strand of quilting thread, no more than 18 inches long. We begin and end each line of stitching by tying a single knot and popping it through the top layer into the batting. Always take several stitches at a time since this will help keep them straight. Stitches should be as small as possible and uniform in size. Quilt in rows, from the center towards the sides.

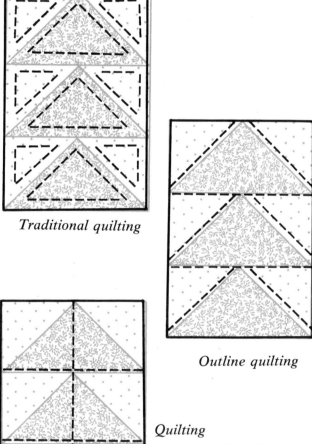

Traditional quilting

Outline quilting

Quilting through the triangles

Quilting the stripe

Binding the Quilt

To make a double layer bias binding, fold the cut edge of the fabric to the selvage. Fold again as shown. Measure and mark the first strip 2 inches from the folds. Continue marking strips every 4 inches. Cut on the marked lines. Join using ½ inch seams and trimming to ¼ inch after pressing them open. Fold the binding in half lengthwise and press. Staystitch the edges together with a ¼ inch seam. Leave the first 10 inches open.

Sew the binding to the three layers of the quilt. Stitch along the design of any outside stripes. Stop the stitching ¼ inch away from the corners. Backstitch one stitch, then raise the needle and presser foot. Form a ½ inch pleat in the binding. Reinsert the needle on the other side of the pleat. Pivot the quilt and continue sewing.

Stop the stitching about 12 inches away from the starting point. Remove some of the staystitching and open the ends. Overlap the ends and mark, allowing for seams. Cut off the excess, then join the ends of the binding. Finish sewing the binding to the quilt. Trim the excess backing but leave an inch of batting to pad the binding. This will help it wear longer. Blindstitch the binding to the back of the quilt.

Some of the smaller items have been finished without a separate binding. These are wall quilts that will never experience the wear that a bed quilt will. Finish these by placing the top and backing right sides together. Machine stitch the edges, leaving an opening for turning. The batting is whipstitched to the edges, then the whole thing is turned right side out. The opening is blindstitched. The outer stripe forms the finishing edge instead of a binding.

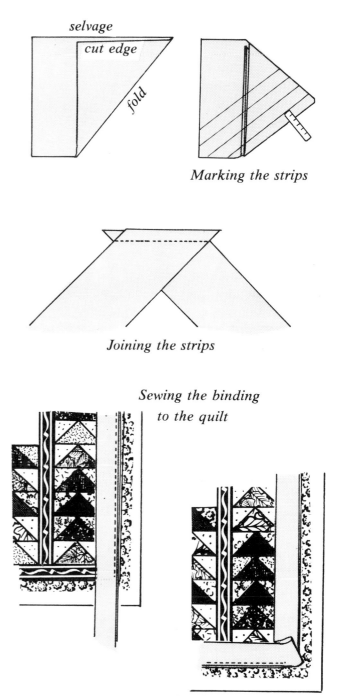

Marking the strips

Joining the strips

*Sewing the binding
to the quilt*

Forming the pleat

Joining the ends

*Stitching the binding
to the quilt back*

Yardage Charts

The first column lists the number of rows of triangles that should be marked across the width of the fabric. The second column lists the actual measurement. The third column lists the amount of fabric to purchase and the fourth column contains the total number of units that amount of fabric will yield.

Divide the total number of units needed by the number of fabrics to be used. This will give the necessary number of units of each. Find this number (or the next larger) in the fourth column on the chart. Refer to the first column for the number of rows to mark, and the third for the amount of fabric to purchase of each. You will need the same amount for both the large triangle and the background triangles.

Yardage Chart (Triangles)

Template size—3″			
Rows	Inches	Yardage	Total Units
1	2	1/8	14
2	4	1/4	28
3	6	1/4	42
4	8	1/3	56
5	10	3/8	70
6	12	3/8	84
7	14	1/2	98
8	16	5/8	112
9	18	5/8	126
10	20	3/4	140

Template size—4″			
Rows	Inches	Yardage	Total Units
1	2-1/2	1/8	12
2	5	1/4	24
3	7-1/2	1/3	36
4	10	3/8	48
5	12-1/2	1/2	60
6	15	1/2	72
7	17-1/2	5/8	84
8	20	5/8	96
9	22-1/2	3/4	108
10	25	7/8	120

Template size—5″			
Rows	Inches	Yardage	Total Units
1	3″	1/8	10
2	6	1/4	20
3	9	3/8	30
4	12	1/2	40
5	15	1/2	50
6	18	5/8	60
7	21	2/3	70
8	24	3/4	80
9	27	7/8	90
10	30	7/8	100
11	33	1	110
12	36	1-1/8	120
13	39	1-1/4	130
14	42	1-1/4	140
15	45	1-3/8	150

We have listed the required number of lengths of stripes for each quilt. In figuring the size of the length, we use the measurement of the longest stripe in the quilt. This allows for seams and mitered corners. In figuring the number of lengths, we include a length for each outside border as well as the lengths separating the rows.

Since we do not know the number of repeats of the stripe you will be using, we have included a chart. The first and second columns list the quilt size and the lengths required. The numbers across the top are the repeats of the stripe across the width of the fabric. Use this chart to figure how many lengths you will need of your striped fabric. (*Example:* If your fabric has four stripes across the width, and you are making a Twin size quilt, you will need 3 lengths of that fabric.)

The Yardage Chart will translate the number of lengths into the amount of fabric required. The first column lists the number of fabric lengths; across the top are the quilt sizes. (*Example:* If you need 3 lengths of fabric for the twin size quilt, you will purchase 8 yards.)

Length Chart (Stripes)

Repeat of Stripes		2	3	4	5	6	7	8	9	10	11	12	13	14	15
Lengths of Stripes															
Wall quilt	**8**	4	3	2	2	2	2	1							
Baby quilt	**8**	4	3	2	2	2	2	1							
Twin size quilt	**12**	6	5	3	3	2	2	2	2	2	2	1			
Double/Queen size quilt	**14**	7	6	4	3	3	2	2	2	2	2	2	2	1	
King size quilt	**15**	8	5	4	3	3	3	2	2	2	2	2	2	2	1

Yardage Chart (Stripes)

Lengths of Fabric	Quilt Size	Wall Quilt	Baby Quilt	Twin Size Quilt	Double/Queen Size Quilt	King Size Quilt
1		1 yd	1-1/2 yds	2-3/4 yds	3-1/8 yds	3-1/4 yds
2		2	2-7/8	5-3/8	6-1/4	6-1/2
3		3	4-1/4	8	9-1/4	9-3/4
4		3-7/8	5-5/8	10-3/4	12-3/8	12-7/8
5		4-3/4	7	13-3/8	15-1/2	16-1/8
6		5-3/4	8-3/8	16	18-1/2	19-3/8
7		6-5/8	9-3/4	18-3/4	21-5/8	22-5/8
8		7-5/8	11-1/8	21-3/8	24-3/4	25-3/8

Wall Quilt

Quilt size—27″ × 34″
Template size—3″
Rows in quilt—5
Units per row—20
Total units—100

Actual size of quilt will vary, depending on width of stripe used.

Lengths of stripes—8
Backing—1-1/4 yards
Binding—3/4 yard
One background fabric—1/2 yard
   (Cut 7 rows)

Total number of fabrics	Number of fabrics 	Amount of each	Rows to cut of each
10	5 / 5	1/4 yard	2
20	10 / 10	1/8 yard	1

Baby Quilt

Quilt size—38″ × 50″
Template size—4″
Rows in quilt—5
Units per row—22
Total units—110

Actual size of quilt will vary, depending on width of stripe used.

Lengths of stripes—8
Backing—1-1/2 yards
Binding—1 yard
One background fabric—7/8 yard
   (Cut 10 rows)

Total number of fabrics	Number of fabrics	Amount of each	Rows to cut of each
12	6 / 6	1/4 yard	2
24	12 / 12	1/8 yard	1

Twin Size Quilt

Quilt size—75″ × 96″
Template size—5″
Rows in quilt—9
Units per row—36
Total units—324

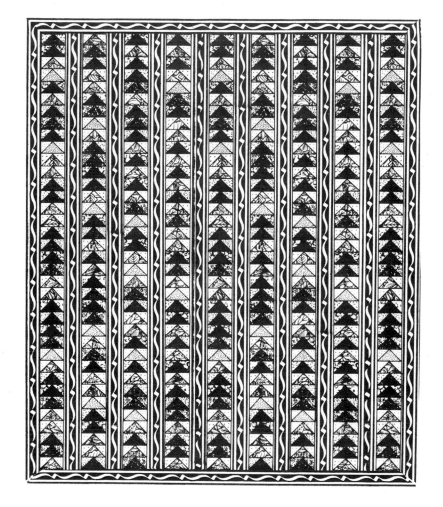

Actual size of quilt will vary, depending on width of stripe used.

Lengths of stripes—12
Backing—5-3/4 yards (2—100″ lengths)
Binding—1-1/2 yards
One background fabric—3 yards
   (Cut 33 rows)

Total number of fabrics	Number of fabrics ◣◢ / ◤◥	Amount of each	Rows to cut of each
20	10 / 10	1/2 yard	4
30	15 / 15	3/8 yard	3
60	30 / 30	1/4 yard	2

Double-Queen Size Quilt

Quilt size—91″ × 111″
Template size—5″
Rows in quilt—11
Units per row—42
Total units—462

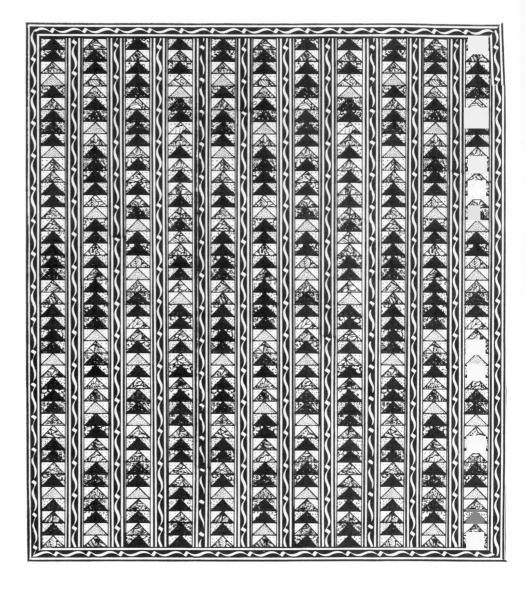

Actual size of quilt will vary, depending on width of stripe used.

Lengths of stripes—14
Backing—9-3/4 yards (3—115″ lengths)
Binding—1-1/2 yards
One background fabric—4 yards
  (Cut 47 rows)

Total number of fabrics	Number of fabrics ◣ / ◺	Amount of each	Rows to cut of each
24	12 / 12	1/2 yard	4
36	18 / 18	3/8 yard	3
60	30 / 30	1/4 yard	2

King Size Quilt

Quilt size—105″ × 116″
Template size—5″
Rows in quilt—12
Units per row—44
Total units—528

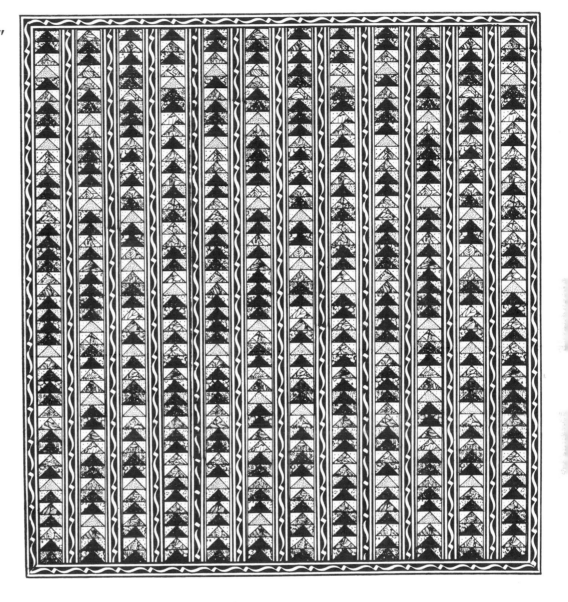

Actual size of quilt will vary, depending on width of stripe used.

Lengths of stripes—15
Backing—10-1/8 yards (3—120″ lengths)
Binding—1-3/4 yards
One background fabric—4¾ yards
(Cut 53 rows)

Total number of fabrics	Number of fabrics		Amount of each	Rows to cut of each
	◣	◺		
24	12 / 12		1/2 yard	5
40	20 / 20		3/8 yard	3
60	30 / 30		1/4 yard	2

Miniature Quilt

Quilt size—15″ × 18″
Unit size—1″ × 2″
Rows in quilt—4
Units per row—15
Total Units—60

1/8 yard of fabric will yield 36 units. Use small pieces or scraps for a variety of fabrics. You will need seven 1/2 yard lengths of stripes.

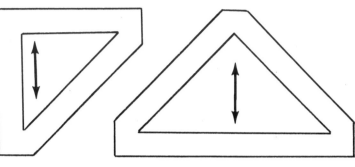

Sashing

Template size—3″

Sashing will frame a 15″ block.
(See Plate 6)

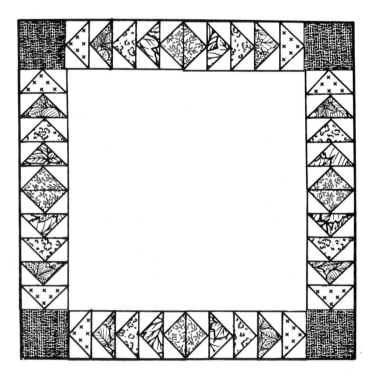

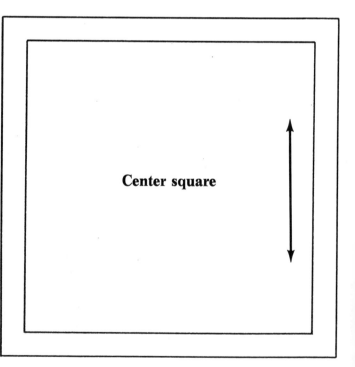

Center square

Wild Goose Chase Block

Block size—10-1/2″
Template size—3″

Each block contains 12 units. Use Center Square pattern or join four large triangles to form the center of the block. Plan a quilt by determining how many blocks are needed then multiplying the number of units in each. Refer to the Yardage Charts for the number of rows to cut and yardage amounts.

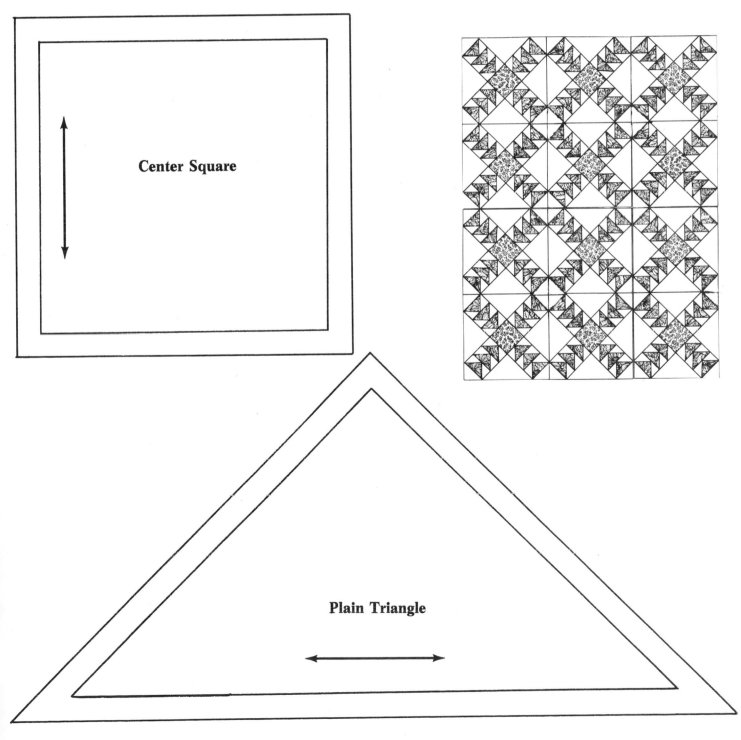

Center Square

Plain Triangle

Wild Goose Chase Quilt

Quilt size—89″ × 108″
Template size—3″
Block size—22-1/4″
Blocks—12
Total units—786
(*A*—441 / *B*—345)

(See Plate 12)

Plain fabric for blocks and borders—3-1/2
  yards
Backing—9-3/8 yards (3—112″ lengths)
Binding—1-1/2 yards

Use these fabrics as shown, or use assorted
scraps in various shades of the three colors.

Fabrics A—This color crosses the block
diagonally.
Fabrics B—This color crosses the block
vertically and horizontally.
Fabrics C—This color forms the background
for all the triangles.

Fabric	Amount	Rows to cut
A	2-1/4 yards	32
B	1-3/4 yards	25
C	3-1/2 yards	56

Diamond—Cut 48 from *Fabrics A*; 48 from *Fabrics B*.

Diamond background—Cut 96 from *Fabrics C*.

Plain triangle—Cut 96 from plain fabric.

Borders—Cut 2 2-1/2″ × 68″; 2 2-1/2″ × 90″
Cut 2 5-1/2″ × 90″; 2 5-1/2″ × 110″

Border Triangle—Cut 4 from *Fabrics B*; 4 from plain fabric.

Cut borders from plain fabric first. Cut plain triangles along the length, then the width of fabric. Construct the blocks as shown.

These yardage amounts include extra fabric for the diamonds.

Square each block by adding a large triangle from *Fabrics A*.

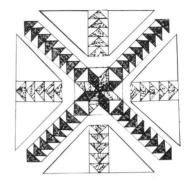

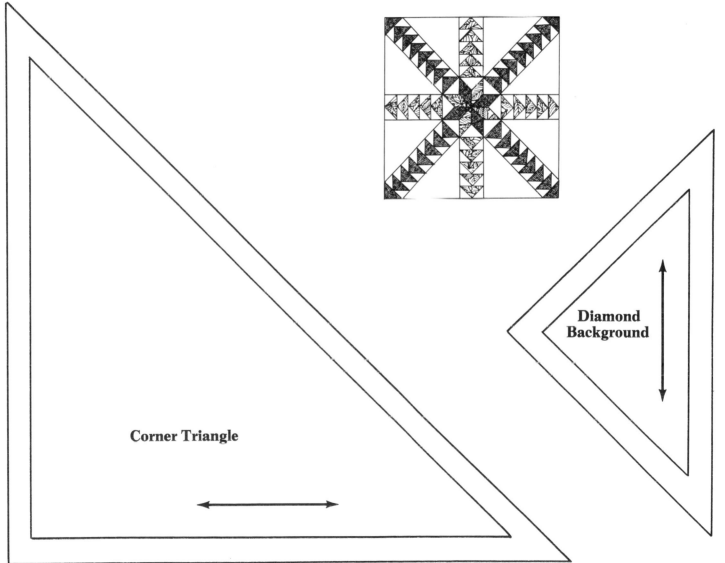

Corner Triangle

Diamond Background

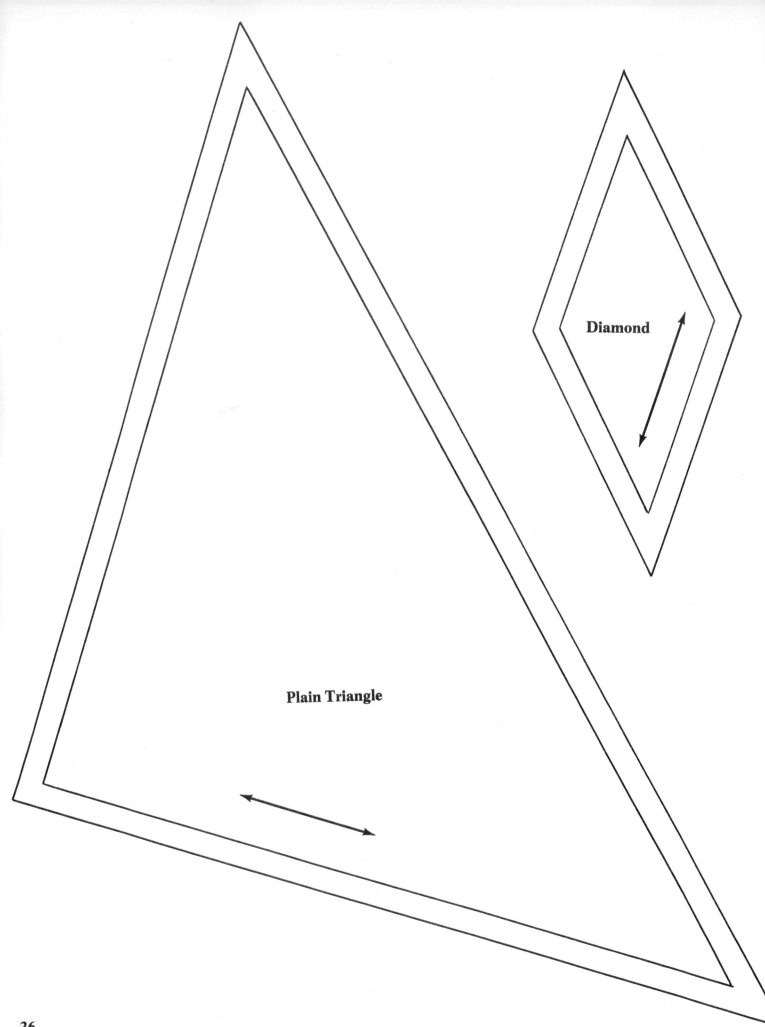

Diamond

Plain Triangle